THE UNWRITTEN WORDS

A Black Woman's Perspective on Life and Love

SEMIRRA M. LONG

authorHOUSE®

AuthorHouse™
1663 Liberty Drive
Bloomington, IN 47403
www.authorhouse.com
Phone: 1 (800) 839-8640

Published by AuthorHouse 02/24/2017

ISBN: 978-1-5246-7322-2 (sc)
ISBN: 978-1-5246-7321-5 (e)

Print information available on the last page.

This book is printed on acid-free paper.

Contents

For my father Rodney Long and all of my fellow survivors;
We live because we have endless light in darkness.

The One

I wish every woman could feel what I'm feeling right now
His eyes, his touch, I never want to come down
At last real love has really been found
He tells me he needs me for life and that one day I'll be his wife
Friend or lover he'll never let go
I'm so happy I didn't let my heart turned cold
What does love feel like? I always wanted to know
Now I do and I'm never ever letting him go

Quiet Night

Be still night
so that I may have a chance to hear my heart beat again
hot tears on a window pane wet from the storm
one day, one day it will return to the norm
a shooting pain within my chest
is it love or just like the rest
if the earth moves would you feel it with me in all this noise?
Can we have a moment or would time stand still?
If only...
Be still night so that I May have the chance to hear my heart beat again

I'm Sorry

I'm Sorry but I can't fix my lips to tell you lies

I'm sorry for the curve of my hips and the jiggle of my thighs

I'm sorry I can't be what you want me to be

I'm sorry all I know how to do is survive

I'm sorry my skin is caramel smooth and not milky white

I'm sorry my hair is curly and brown, everything you claim you don't like

I'm sorry I express myself with this pen and don't brag or boast

I'm sorry my son died before he got to live

I'm sorry many Black males have this as their reality

I'm sorry that we lose them

I'm sorry this is the story of most

I'm sorry I always give more than I get

I'm sorry but I had to get these words off my chest

I'm sorry but I'm just me I'm just doing my best

Echo

If sound resounds it can emulate everything I hear when I wake
The sound of the needle scratching as the record plays
The memory of you I can never erase
Silent pain amongst a sea of smiles
My heart echoes the memories of being a child
If I scream from this mountaintop would they hear me?
Or would my voice echo then fade into silence until you are near me
If sound resounds it can emulate everything I hear when I wake
The sound of my echo could make the world shake

Return to Love

Although you're not with me I can always feel you
with each sound that echoes I wish I could hear you
my day is long, my life is blessed
every night you give me rest
the timbre in your voice like a calm wind to my life
if I could than all I would do is write...about the way you make me laugh
the gentle way you make everything right
how no other man is in my sight
how it all feels like a dream
how I wish that you were here with me
they could take all I have
as long as I have you there's not a day I would be sad
another chance to feel your lips and for your fingertips to graze my hips
I never knew love could feel like this

Black Lives Matter

I want to heal all the hurts that you feel
to have your son ricocheted with bullets, that can't be real
this is all starting to remind me of Emmett Till
what's the value of a Black life is it 3/5ths still or is there none?
live in peace and still die by the gun
hands up, don't shoot
burn down our own, rob and loot
what in the name of Sandra Bland do we have here
more shots fired, more Black tears
if all lives matter why are we the only ones dying
if the protest is wrong and its Kapernicks jersey you're burning
bring back Trayvon, Mike Brown, Eric Garner, Philando Castile and
Alton Sterling
Malcolm said they would resist every time we raise our Black fist
scream Black lives matter and they get pissed
Michelle told us to go high
every week we getting hit can you tell me why
if a Black life has value and a Black life matters
Just wake me up when the bloodshed no longer splatters

Until the World Ends

One day soon you'll hold me close and I'll feel your touch
there's so much I want to say, but words don't seem like enough
in a world that hates I just want to love
if tomorrow the world should end I'll be content to feel this way again

Above the Clouds (for Dequan)

I used to have a fear of flying until he took me above the clouds with
his wings
if there were words for this I could probably more easily explain
to transport my soul to another place I'd gladly run every mile of this race
I used to have a fear of flying until he took me above the clouds with
just his wings
if time were to pass and we come face to face
I'd mark the day as the day I saw heaven

Unrequited (for Lydell)

I don't care for carefree connections
love is not a guarantee but always a blessing
choosing to vibrate higher and seeking self first
still nothing ever prepares or protects you from the hurt
when love enters it can liberate enhance and set free
but to have it taken away is the part we dread the most
to love again after heartbreak becomes so hard to see
I don't care for carefree connections but I love to have you in my space
if it were up to me I'd have the chance to love you everyday
but since I can't force it or make things exist
I'll just wait patiently for your love and everlasting kiss.

Little Girl Lost (For 8 year Old Me)

Little Girl Lost-you're way too pretty to see such ugly things
the way daddy drinks while the radio sings
the hardwood floor creaks at night
he's outside your door, get ready to fight
he comes in to take your innocence
somewhere else daddy's still drinking, this makes no sense
you smile so pretty and everyone tells you you're cute
you spend your whole life with your voice on mute
you can never tell he has a gun
if you tell mama she will take off and run
you dance and sing to find your voice
write things down you have no choice
little girl lost you're way too pretty to see such ugly things
it's ok to tell now and let your voice ring

Did I Entertain You?

Did I entertain you when I told you I loved you
how about now when I place no one above you?
If God Himself were to tell me it's time
I would wish for one more minute to make you mine
Did I entertain you when I cried
punched and kicked the air and screamed out of fright?
would you be there in the morning or Leave in the black of night?
was it funny to you to make me feel like a fool?
Or were you sad too, did I leave your life misty blue?
Love is not a game and I'm not a clown on your stage
But I hope I entertain you when I turn and walk away

A Letter to My Mother

Mama I know you're tired

Mama I know you're sick

But I've got some words for you and I need you to hear this

Am I what you traded for a life so sweet?

Did you leave me to rot like week old meat?

Was his love worth trading my body and soul?

Did you hear me when I cried for you in the dark and light?

Could you hear him coming in my bedroom on those cold late nights?

Mama can you hear me now when I tell you I just needed you

To tell me you value me more than the cars, house and all the jewels

I suffered greatly but nothing hurt more than you calling me a liar

But mama I must thank you cause you set my soul on fire

Never will I let a man come before my child

Mama you can't run from me now so you mind as well sit down awhile

For too long I've been silent but I'm speaking now so I need you to be quiet

I've written this letter to my mother but you were never that to me

now I've gotten these words out and my soul has finally been set free!

Loveless World

It is the greatest gift to love and most have taken it for granted
In a world gone crazy love is disenchanted
Hearts are raked over hot, black coals
Everybody giving it up but giving nothing, let the truth be told
men act like lovers without any souls
Cheating and lying to protect themselves
Hurt running so deep they don't want it to be felt
Women offering their bodies and not much else
Because when we give our hearts too many feelings are felt
For some women like me who already love themselves
We just want the chance to give our love to somebody else
A world without love will surely cease to exist
But maybe we can change the world with just a simple kiss

The Kiss

I don't remember all your words

my memory fails at times

I do recall your eyes, how brown they shine in the light

I hold back just a little when I get in your presence

if you truly knew how you made me feel there would be no second guessing

they say to know how he feels you have to read his kiss

I swear I transport through time each time I feel your lips

when I try to pull away

you always pull me back in to tell me that I'm safe

the joy It brings to touch your lips with mine is so close to God I think

I'll call it divine

In this moment, with this kiss I am yours and you are mine

Made to Order

Like your favorite drink at Starbucks
Carmel Macchiato with a hint of espresso
If you ask I'll never tell you no
to stop the world outside our window
rejuvenate and mix souls until it all makes sense
we can't stop until we reach heaven
they try to stop your majesty but the king in you all can see
while everyone has got the blues we just keep on loving endlessly

Black women don't wear weaves because we are insecure, want to be White, hate ourselves. Some women wear weaves for health reason, expression or for variety of styles without damaging our natural hair.

My Hair

I'm not sorry for my hair
I'm not sorry for the many styles I wear
Bonding, glue or stitching
The way it's worn, it's not a contradiction
If my hair weave offends you, please tell me why?
It's not something I wear to cover up inside
There are times I let my own hair flow and smile with pride
my hair, my hair
Don't whisper, don't stare
Braids, twists, weaves and locs
I love ALL the styles that I rock
You call me a sellout because of my expression?
Last time I checked we share a complexion
My hair, my hair
it never let my soul leave
And since you're not buying it don't worry about my weave!

Queen

From greatness you come
the curve of your hips, lips and then some
the mother of earth and all that we see
who am I talking about? Must be those Black Queens
the backbone of a nation and race
for all the indescribable pain and suffering we face
A king rules but he's nothing without his Queen
She rises, stands tall, there is no in between
from the thrones and pyramids to cotton fields and plantations
the Jim Crow south, black invention, education and first lady leading
the nation
Everywhere you look you see a Queen
She is you, you and you
She is me

My Brother (for Rashad)

My brother, sweet brother I feel your pain
my brother, little brother I see your strain
if I had one wish I would feel it for you and take it away
In like a storm of torrential wind and rain
It makes no sense but still we pray
Another obstacle on your course I'm sure you will defeat
the blood of kings flowing
through your veins, fire under your feet
when you were born you looked at me with your big hazel eyes
I want you to remember that the sun will always rise
we know adversity but we don't know defeat
my brother my brother you soon will be set free
#DefeatEpilepsy

Convalescent Heart

I gave you poetry, you gave me pain
But you also Gave me rest amidst the strain
A calming wind you were in the middle of the the storms and strife
But the day you left almost ended my life
Recovery road has been bumpy, can barely stand on my feet
I sometimes pray that you'll come back to me
Never had a man bring me to my knees
And where I felt without him I wasn't complete
It's time to let go now and get back to living
I thank you for the lesson and the love that you have given

There has never been a more crucial election in recent American history. As a Black person in America I will never forget the struggles of my people as I stated in a previous status yesterday. I am grateful, I thank you all and although this is my first year not voting with my grandma I will be there to exercise my right. Thank you Barack Obama, you gave us hope in a time of hopelessness and proved a Black man CAN change the world!

Vote or Die (Inspired by the 2016 Presidential election)

I can't believe the things I hear
so many have shocked me as the election draws near
"I'm not voting, they don't care about us"
I live in the hood so why make a fuss?
whoever gets in they will only take care of the rich
I can't even say I disagree with this
But the billy clubs cracking the souls of my people is my motivation
In case you forgot we are nothing without representation
they say we are lazy and you plan on proving them right?
I wonder how some of you sleep at night
the long walks to vote in worn down shoes with no soles
attack dogs and nearly drowning from the water of a fire hose
Sit ins and "nigger shut up" you don't have any rights
Marching in Selma, dying and souls taking flight
"This election is pointless I'll just close my eyes"
But what if our people never fought for your rights?
Sit down and settle and have no voice
don't pull that lever, it's really your choice
As tribute and duty to those before me I'll also sacrifice
come rain, hail, sleet or snow I'm going to vote or die!

Depression touched us all at some point in time. Life is funny and immensely beautiful but sadness is a realistic part of it. To those needing a little light in their dark, I see you, I am you and together we can have hope and live on our brightest path.

Blue

The people I talked to daily have no time for me now
when You're feeling down nobody wants you around
the black hole swallows you up and spits you out
you cry, sleep, scream and shout
but nobody is there to listen...
"I've got my own problems" and "I have to take care of my kids"
no one is there to wipe your tears, just the moonlight where they glisten
it enters like a thief in the night taking you under
where the real you went people start to wonder
too much pain not enough release
it comes and knocks you right off your feet
tell me a time when you met my friend blue
I'm sure you've met him a time or two
the thing about him is he never stays
and when he leaves there are only sunny days

American Tragedy

New trees but the same strange fruit

Now they make laws instead of hanging us from the noose

Black man, black man why are you so feared?

That they would take your life in cold blood without shedding one tear

Thugs, gangsters and criminals

The names they call you has no minimum

But what if I told you it's all a lie?

That the Black man is strong and humble and shy

That it started by separating him from his children and wife

And by taking his religion he was stripped of his way of life

The American tragedy is that we were bought and sold

And we are forced to listen to all the lies that have been told

Now instead of lynching and swinging from a tree

We have to work twice as hard in this land, we ain't free

Black man, black man you are the original

Stand on the shoulders of this backwards nation, let their message remain subliminal

You are not what they say you are, you are visionaries and achievers

The true American tragedy is that we have to turn them all into believers

I'm Still Here

Many people ask why I write poetry
You would too if you've seen the things I've seen
The mind collapsing of your mother
Getting fed up, taking it out on you and your brothers
Your daddy drinks but loves you so much
Your stepdad violates you with bad touch
Kids call you names because you're intelligent
It took years to know that they're irrelevant
Why do I write?
Because of all the feelings I have inside
They are too painful to try to hide
I listened to rappers and how they rhymed
About their hard lives, just like mine
When I was 13 I tried to take my life
I'm sad to say that wasn't the last time
But I prayed to God then and I do now
He kept me here, it wasn't time to go out
The pain I had I thought no one could feel
But I am strong and I am real
I had to let go and feel no fear
I may not be perfect but I'm still here

Chocolate Smile

Black woman I know you're stressed
Black woman I know you're depressed
A little Brown girl with braids and beads
You had no cares or responsibility
Now the stress of the world is on your shoulders
I'm sad to say it's part of getting older
So many assume things about you by your looks
They may think you twerk but not read books
Or that you steal and not earn money
In the stores where they look at you funny
And the workplace where you are overlooked
And the men that mistreat you after they dig in their hooks
The hardships and hurdles at every turn
Drowning your pain in bottles as your cigarette burns
Shaking and twisting, screaming and shouting
But the Black woman is strong right, no time for doubting
Or your hot angry tears that supply enough water for Flint
The sons we bury because of our environment
The mistreatment and abuse
Hiding and stuffing our pain with food
Black woman sit and rest a while
It's time for the world to see your chocolate smile

The Backbone

The uprising in America is not a new idea
Ku Klux Klan, Jim Crow and slavery all started here
Because our skin is Black you tell us what we lack
Or what you think we do but we know it's not fact
We built this country on our backs
Enforced laws to tell us where to sit, ride the bus and eat
To not be called a nigger, that was a treat
But when Huey and Stockley told us to take pride
It seems that the Klan took an extra ride
Black power doesn't mean anti- white
The Panthers started WIC and taught us all how to fight
With knowledge of laws and self -defense
Not going around telling white people how much we hate them
The difference is we uplift and seize
While they hated and bombed us, lynched us from trees
The Black man loved himself and his woman
The community was clean with no pollutants
The backbone of our progress were the teachings of Garvey, Martin
and Malcolm
Black youth were educated by them and happy to have found them
I thank my dad for all his knowledge
For encouraging me to go to college
The backbone of the progress of our race
Can't come from t.v., we must relearn how to educate

The Struggle

If I can make the money that I make here for someone else
Imagine the money that I can make for myself
To use the talent of Young Black minds to build their wealth
But to starve our potential and keep it all to themselves
The biggest mind game in all the land
To use me then discard me because I'm not a white man
The pain I feel everyday here I can barely describe
But I will try to in this poem, line by line
When I was quiet they found ways to say I was too silent
I spoke up and they said I was violent
Tried to fire me for something I did not even say
Labeled me a racist and stopped my pay
Giving me "women's work" day in and day out
The boredom makes people do things they never would
All of this aggravation just to stay out the hood
My frustrations aren't understood by most here
This is what I was writing about when I wrote "Black Tears"
I only know how to channel my emotions with a pen
I will never work so hard for Corporate America Again
Don't tell me the money is worth it and just be silent
By now we all know that I am done being quiet
I will take my brain power and use it for myself
The struggle I have many can't relate to
To go to a job and complain I have to be a fool
But what we are given doesn't have to be accepted
This struggle I face it may be a blessing

Lifetime Love

They say love doesn't exist anymore and most people are fake
Who are "they", why does their opinion hold weight?
A lifetime love is something we all want
A real King or Queen to show off and flaunt
Where your souls are connected and hearts aligned
And in every life I am yours and you are mine
The World wants to kill off the Gods and Earths
But me I can't wait for the day I give birth
To our young prince or princess
The dream will be complete and my life will be set
Like in Ancient Egypt, Greece, Rome and in slavery
I always had you but I want more than your baby
To look in your eyes every day and to see your smile
That's worth more to me than all the jewels at the bottom of the Nile
To hold your hand through good times and the umbrella through
the storms
A lifetime love is special, not the norm
Although I've known you before in other times
This lifetime is special, our love is divine

Dreams

You can close your eyes or leave them open
When we dream our hopes are spoken
The wheels in our head spins out pictures
Colors and people, a life we envision
Dreams can be had standing, laying down or sitting
The little Black girl who dreams of being a doctor, lawyer or teacher
Sometimes we replay the message we heard from the preacher
Dreams are real important and Langston told us never to forget them
We must remember so we can manifest them
Your dreams are different than mine, we all have our own
Some wish on stars in fields, some in their beds at home
Never stop dreaming and wishing on stars
Dreams are what make us beautiful and how we become who we are

The Great Pretender

With long strides and kicks and shuffles of his feet
The Great Pretender is silent and meek
He comes and goes as he pleases
He prays to anyone Buddha, Allah and Jesus
He hides his emotions with his dance
He'll dance all night if you give him the chance
He smiles and jives
Grins and taps
He keeps going until all the stress is off his back
He spins and twirls forgetting all his struggles
Can't stop now so his footwork doubles
The clown he is to so many that surround him
If given the chance they would surely drown him
In the waves of oppression, seas of doubt and rainfall of hate
The time for pretending is out of date
So dance with him and forget yourself
Or come to know your history and all its wealth
Can't dance anymore because there's no more music
When we stop pretending it's living we're choosing

Little Sister's Song

Let me tell you about loss
Paying your mother's debts at no cost
Starving your body and feeding your spirit
Singing so loud that God Allah could hear it
Everything you're made of remains to be seen
You can cry and scream but must not allow defeat
We don't choose love, it can only choose us
But sit for a while, don't be in a rush
Your dreams and hopes are waiting for you
I love to see you smile and never want to see you blue
So take some time to heal your heart and spirit
But don't stop pushing, allow the pain, don't fear it
What you think you've lost is really a blessing
Your story and song will be your hardest lesson
Look to Him and leave doubt and defeat for the rest
I tell you what I've learned and always wish you the best
You're going to make it just take it all in stride
Just sing your song and smile, life is just beginning and it's a beautiful ride!

Sista

Sista look how the world treats you
But sista you can change how they see you
Do you not realize that you are Black Gold?
That you don't have to believe the lies you've been told?
You are not just a nice backside
you are a warrior, show some pride
your mind is your strength use it until it hurts
don't value yourself on how well you can twerk
bend over, get low, show all you've got
sista, my Black sista don't let your potential rot
hottentot venus we have plenty of those
do men only value you when you take off your clothes?
your crown is heavy, your heart is broken
in boardroom meetings where you are the token
in stores where you are followed and assumed to be broke
for all the times they laughed at the proper English you spoke
for carrying the weight of the world, no time for your own struggles
to get paid less but the workload is double
Sista, my sista I feel your pain
but sista, my Black sista never forget the royal blood in your veins

S.T.R.E.T.C.H.

The practices of meditation and yoga are ancient and unlimited in healing power for any ailment especially depression and anxiety. I am particular to Dahn Yoga but any release is a good one.

I want you to reach as high as you can
Stretch and suspend, let your body bend
Forget who's watching or looking
Let go of the day from beginning to end
Find a focus for a few minutes
Clear your mind, let it go without limits
People love to see you down but they aren't your focus right now
listen to your breath and move accordingly
when you S. T. R. E. T. C. H it's you that you will see !
(Stop, think, relax, evaluate, thank, collect, heal)

Remember (Back in the Day)

Saturday morning cartoons
eating cereal with the biggest spoon
scrunchies to match your fluorescent top
MTV blaring videos, rock and pop
NY winters sledding with my brother down the biggest hill
Boston summers, riding roller coasters for the thrill
manhunt and spin the bottle
Back when I used to sing, dance and model
When crack and cocaine destroyed our communities
and the only thing left to do was practice unity
the street...s were soaked with mother's tears
gangs and violence instilled fear
young, Black and gifted we were taught who we are
but in those days that thought seemed so far
I remember a childhood full of laughter
I wish my book could stop at this chapter
back in the day, a place I'll never forget
I learned to love life, was the teacher's pet
an unordinary life it turned out to be
but give me those days reading books under a tree
or Oregon trail in the 4th grade
mall madness, easy bake oven; with my aunt Diane at Sesame Place
no childhood is perfect or without pain
and I would give anything to go back in the day

King of Hearts

Everyday I wake I'm honored to be in your presence
Even when you're away, I can still feel your essence
I let my guard down only with you
You're there for me when I'm smiling or blue
It's been a short time, only 2 1/2 years
But there were countless kisses and you wiped my tears
The way you heal me with your touch and your words
It's soul shaking and stirring, I feel like we're in our own world
I wouldn't trade any of it, the ups and the downs
You falling in love with her or me walking out
No matter what we come back to each other
I will never find a greater friend or lover
You pursue your dreams relentlessly and work so hard
But you take time to love me, you're the king of hearts

Black Tears

The hot sun beated down on the heads of the field slaves
Picking cotton, building and digging their child's graves
Escape routes and buying their freedom if they were brave
The crack of the whip in the cold, crisp air
Where our people were beaten and life wasn't fair
Now we've built this country on our backs, sweat pouring from our brows
And raised slave master's children without any frowns
Secretly read, prayed to Allah and Jesus/Invented soul food, a new way to feed us
The mind of an African, naturally full of wit and intelligence
Transported to a land where we have no relevance
Fast forward to Jim Crow and fighting for our rights
Lynchings and bombings, KKK riding at night
Why are we feared in a land where we're oppressed?
Where you mock our features in cartoons and on your television sets
Black women in videos shaking their asses
When the slave master stole our virtue with rape and gave out passes
Too Black or not Black enough, no unity just division
Arguing and yelling but expecting respect to be given
Internal rage that other races will never understand
The earth is soaked with the tears of both the Black woman and Black man

Woman Woes

Her tears are plentiful flooding oceans and lakes
The pain of a woman, how her heart breaks
In a country that questions everything she says
And if she works instead of motherhood it's "off with her head"
Most women do both now, balancing career with mommyhood
Would give their children the world if only they could
A woman is the giver of life, who wouldn't be for her?
But in this nation we call her slut, thot and worst of all whore
The disrespect comes in waves these days
But woman will be woman and her head will raise
And hopefully one day we can say that about her working wage
And a woman President will be on the front page
And her rights won't be attacked and she'll no longer get raped
These woman woes we've all got them
But only men have the power to respect us and to stop them

Conditional Love

Your love is conditional it comes with many rules
your love isn't smart but only for fools
You say I want what you have?
What exactly do I lack?
The lying and cheating part? Please don't make me laugh
Because someone is next to you with a warm body doesn't mean their
heart is too
The energy of a person you claim had better be pure and true
Don't tell me you're unhappy behind closed doors then change
Please be real with yourself, we're getting too old to be fake
Love isn't conditional if it's real and true
But before you can look for love baby girl, you've got to love you

The Wakeup

My grandfather was born the same day as Dr King died
The 4th day of April, 5 days before mine
Government took him out like they did Malcolm
The melanin you have is worth more than talcum
Don't be fooled by who they put in power
Allah has strength mightier than any tower
Your body parts they are for sale
Do you wonder why or even care?
Wake up and rise up Black people, remove your veils

Gods and Earths

Islam is not violence or what you see on t.v.
120 lessons, Supreme math and alphabet are what we teach
The joy I get from the Gods I've met
Reminds me of our other lives when we connect
My value as an earth I never knew
The Gods, Black men are the foundation
The earths, Black women, responsible for creation
A nation that knows no holidays
We still gather with family and celebrate
Enlightened truth setters
Doctors, lawyers, teachers, rappers all go getters
To spread the knowledge is our duty
Without putting you on trial, without a jury
The true essence of Blackness and who you are
Asiatic Black men and Beautiful Black stars
The Gods, the Earths we are the way, truth and light
Following the lessons your wrongs become right
Allah is you and you are Him/But we are still human, not without sin
G originally meant God and not a gangsta
The earths were made in his image to give you life, you should thank us

The Price

much is your soul worth?
Could you handle being sold by your mother at birth?
Baptized in the Nile of denial
Nobody speaks
Witnessing your brutal rape but cash is king so they pretend not to see
Swirling thoughts of a tragic life
Where You're told this is your husband, he thinks you're his wife
what you thought you saw was just an illusion
Never look at me and draw conclusions
Bumping my head against brick walls to forget
I thought I was special but I was just a bet
Used, thrown out and hung out to dry
the days marked in tears as time goes by
They paid my fee and stole my life
and I'm the one that pays the price

Warrior

They say behind every powerful man a strong woman sits
enough pain and torture to consider slitting wrists
brown as the earth, black like dirt
we scream and shout so the world hears our hurt
off slave ships and born free
Power streaming from the fist of an Ethiopian queen
We bear the load and get no reward
Fight until death with words, action and swords
the warrior woman can never be over looked
her strength and regalness, her stunning good looks
to not know your history and from where you came
you're giving away all your power in this game
she is a mother, teacher, wife, daughter and sister
She prefers you call her anything but a quitter
ask a warrior woman why she fights
she will tell you it's her way and it's her right

I Didn't Ask You

I didn't ask you to stay
I never wanted you to go
I wanted you to be free
not put your life on hold
the damage we suffered separately brought hope
that I could drink from your cup and cope
the poisons of the past ate away at us both
I ran from your spirit, your demons, your black cloak
When I was breathless and drowning in tears
nightmares and anxiety of suffering, abuse for years
you didn't leave my heart unattended
I didn't ask you/but somehow you knew
that life was swallowing me whole
and what I was dealing with I couldn't handle alone
and the people around me they couldn't hold my hand
and fuck love you don't need me and I don't need a man
when the night ran into day
and our love was still the same
and the loss that we suffered we can never again gain
I didn't ask you but you're here
I'll never turn your love away in smiles or tears

Funky Dysfunction

I know how Pink felt when she wrote "Family Portrait"
My family is a mess, my family is a trip
Screaming, yelling at the top of their lungs
With the backdrop of soul music and the pulsating African drum
drugs and drinking
my daddy's record player scratches the record as he's thinking
mom off her meds again, my brother in his crib crying
me sitting in my bedroom window, my soul slowly dying
Everyone has dysfunction or so they say
But... if you were on this team you would never want to play
the lying and crying gets too much for me
but after all these years I'm finally setting me free
Because I love from a distance if at all
Won't get a text, email or even a phone call
Got Prince, MJ and Stevie as the soundtrack to our pain
My family function is dysfunctional but funky, smooth like rain
It is what is and ain't no changing it
That funky dysfunction; But every record played won't be a hit

American Tragedy

New trees but the same strange fruit

Now they make laws instead of hanging us from the noose

Black man, black man why are you so feared?

That they would take your life in ...cold blood without shedding one tear

Thugs, gangsters and criminals

The names they call you has no minimum

But what if I told you it's all a lie?

That the Black man is strong and humble and shy

That it started by separating him from his children and wife

And by taking his religion he was stripped of his way of life

The American tragedy is that we were bought and sold

And we are forced to listen to all the lies that have been told

Now instead of lynching and swinging from a tree

We have to work twice as hard in this land, we ain't free

Black man, black man you are the original

Stand on the shoulders of this backwards nation, let their message remain subliminal

You are not what they say you are, you are visionaries and achievers

The true American tragedy is that we have to turn them all into believers

Native Daughter

The land we walk on is sacred and historic
We hear many stories of ancestors, the people before us
The cry of the eagle as he hovers and protects
A culture that celebrates the elderly and gives them respect
An oral history of parables and fables
Told around fires and dinner tables
The mark of our heritage the letter "M" on your palm
Crooked, flat noses and slanted eyes, internal calm
Native daughters are taught to be respected
Family and duties must never be neglected
Respect the earth and the people here
Pray to Source both with a smile and with tears
We are not savages or a costume
The land was stolen but still it blooms
Now our voices are heard as we fight for our rights
Native daughters and sons we only know how to unite
She is more than beautiful hair, cheekbones and skin
The native daughter has the spirit of the wolf within

I Don't Know

I don't know why life gives me so much pain and strife

Or why I and so many people around me have tried to take their lives

While I haven't felt that way in quite some time because I channel my
emotions when I write

I can write a poem so beautiful you would never know I hurt so deeply

That my pillow is soaked with tears at night and I pace my bedroom
floor that's so creaky

The abuse and trauma, loss and fear

Every time I close my eyes, the memories are near

I've done the work and healed my heart

You only see my smile in the light, not my frown in the dark

My words are unwritten because I still have life to live

But I just don't know why it is the way it is

I don't know the answers or why Allah tests me so greatly

When He took my childhood, my friends lives and my baby

I do know that I have strong faith and I am brave

I won't give up, I'll face the day

I don't know the answers but I do have some questions

I don't know how to deal with this, do you have any suggestions?

Black Girl Magic

She's culture personified, the glow of her skin, the steps in her stride
Her magic is her power it drips from her fingertips
The Black man is mesmerized by the curve of her hips and her lips
Her influence is great, she can change the world
She's a mother, wife, sister and somebody's little girl
When we see her time seems to stop
Can't keep our eyes off of her or the fashion she rocks
CEO, salon owner, doctor, teacher and in the White House
Her magic is her own, she is a compliment to her spouse
Black girl, black girl she isn't your stereotype
Not a welfare recipient, not just a mother and wife
The original woman with melanin that shines bright
This Black Girl magic, we've got it for life!

Black History

The history of our people has deep and strong roots
Marches that were peaceful, combat without the boots
America, the land where they teach only what they want you to know
And bury the facts that we have uncovered and now show
The crack of the whip on the slaves that built this nation
That's the only image we are shown, of our greatness we had no indication
The freedom fighters, Garvey, Malcolm and Martin
We all know their contributions and way of thinking they started
But before these leaders we were indigenous to this place
The raping and trading of our people, what a disgrace
To have a history so rich and beautiful that it was stolen
And the people, me and you, us we are so broken
Our discoveries and contributions, there are plenty
The history has been hidden but the truth seekers, there are so many
History, history it's one in the same
But if you look in the mirror and don't know yourself, who is to blame?

The Exchange

They say Black love is dead and gone

That Black men use us, we are only a pawn

To look at the big picture, I might say "they" are right

If I didn't know my people, all our strength and all our might

The trickle down of chattel slavery effects

Where the Black man was raped too and Black women used to warm beds

Don't wonder why our community is so broken

Why we ignore it and certain words aren't spoken

Being a player or pimp, throwing cash in... a strip club aren't new ideas

The slave owner taught you that, we've been pimped for years

If you think you're getting over by bedding many women

And taking advantage of the gift you've been given

Of the beautiful body of the original woman

Her struggles she looks to rid of with you that would remain hidden

Never take for granted the exchange she gives you

On days she's beaten by the world and her life's a little blue

Our people suffer greatly but loving comes naturally

The exchange shouldn't be abused, Queens value your Kings; Kings please value us Queens

Broken Pieces

I stumbled upon a lecture by Iyanla Vanzant
I seemed to have made up my mind but not my heart yet
To forgive all the abuse and pain
The nights I was abandoned, the days left out in the rain
I can still feel the cold tiles of the kitchen floor
Every time I tried to escape and couldn't take anymore
How his hand would muffle my words and cries
How sometimes I would lay there and wish to die
It was one too many times I watched my mother lose her mind
As the time passed, I came very close to losing mind
The open wounds were washed over with salt water and stung
I prayed God would save me, that the horror would become fun
It never ended for me until I had the courage to leave
But in many ways, I still wasn't free
Until that day I heard that message about peace from broken pieces
How life can give us struggles but we don't have to be them
With faith, belief and strength we can beat them
Like a shattered glass on that cold, tile kitchen floor
I picked up my pieces, I am broken no more

No More Fear

No Matter who you voted for
You have to agree the outcome was poor
A man so intent on taking away the rights of women
Who are all responsible for the life he was given
To threaten government interruption in Chicago when guns already
caused so much destruction
How can these possibly be his solutions?
Pipelines on sacred land of my Native people that cause pollution
No man shall have this much distortion and still succeed
I have no worries in this life you see
Because he can try to take away everything humane we have gained
But none of this will count on judgement day
When we hear the horn blow and God Allah makes His descent
It will no longer matter who is President

The Great Divide

by Semirra Long & Michael J. Falotico

This world of mine it has such a great divide, but image the beauty when poets collide...

Does it matter that I am Black and you are White?

We all need peace and my eyes are open wide, let's march towards harmony and make our future

bright.

My eyes close but it doesn't change the view

The world has a crack that's reaching my heart too...

The cries for peace fall silent on these days

My pen still scribbles with a soul that weeps today...

I Am the Dream

When I wrote about dreams everyone could relate it seems
How we close our eyes and envision
See the pictures in our mind, clear and with precision
They teach you in school about the man who dreamed out loud
Martin Luther King Jr., we say his name and are proud
He wanted us all to be equal and have the same rights
To challenge ourselves, to stand up and fight
Today we are accomplishing what was never expected
Dr. King is smiling down from... heaven
When you look in the mirror you can see it manifest
How we walk with pride and stick out our chests
Earning degrees, high paying jobs and owning Black business
The dream is just starting, it is not yet finished
Dr. King originated many things we see
Just like him we can be anything we want to be
The next time you doubt yourself or what you can be
Look at yourself and say, "I am the dream"!

The End of last year forever changed life as I know it when my dad went into a coma. My best friend, first teacher and one of the greatest writers I know had me see him in a capacity I wasn't yet ready to but I am ready for the total healing and restoration of him. Everyday I pray to have my daddy back and wish for a miracle anyday now. I read this to him at his bedside numerous times and he opened his eyes and smirked. I know he heard it and I know he will fight hard to get back to me and the rest of his family.

While You Were Sleeping (for my dad Rodney L. Long)

I want so much to find some words
for all the years of pain, loss and hurt
to describe this life for people like us, God himself is the only person
we trust
If he were a person at all, He would be like one of us
To come from the ghetto and make a beautiful life
Most would say you had it right
But I have caught your tears and given you hugs
Listened to your lectures about loving thugs
to read and know my culture, be as smart as can be
To not be like the rest of the girls, to close my eyes and dream
The person that I call when I'm happiest or broken
To a girl or woman, her dad's words must be spoken
My first teacher, the person that made me feel like I was great
I wrote this while you were sleeping and can't wait for you to wake

Solstice

The crisp air signals the start of winter
the clock moves back effecting mom, dad, brother and sister
Transition and change come naturally
The leaves have fallen from every tree you see
Ice and snow are the weather of the season
Shopping malls are bustling at the seams for no reason
"Buy this and buy that" are all we hear on t.v.and radio
Few take the time to take in the beauty of nature high and low
It signifies a time for reflection
Most people dread winter because of the temperature decrease
Solstice is beauty and it is a time of peace

The Loss

One of life's greatest miracles was taken from me
It wasn't the time or place apparently
Many people can understand losing their child
After they have grown and stayed awhile
But to lose a life before it gets to start
This right here is the hardest part
Your daddy cried and I slipped into the black abyss
I wanted to hold you and give you kiss after kiss
It gets easier some days and some nights I'm awake like this
I think of this Kwanzaa and all of the gifts
The love we would have given you
The gray skies you could have turned blue
I still smile at your name for you would have been great
My sweet baby boy now you're at heaven's gate
A loss so big only Allah knows why
I will think of you every time I look up at the sky

Open Mic

What right does any man have to tell me how to feel?
The things I find attractive, the qualities that have appeal
That warm touch that's supposed to comfort me
And have the sweetness of a thousand honey bees
Now feels like their sting as they swarm and attack me
My face hitting cold, hard tile
Maybe I should just lay here awhile
But I gather my mind and gather my notebook
A genuine outlet for all the pain I took
When I stand on stage and spew my rhyme
The spotlight that's on me is not all that shines
I shake and stammer but my words are heard
That open mic is mine, I live for spoken word

God and The Devil

In this life where I have known pain
And troubles pour down like an everlasting rain
When I drop to me knees and to Allah I pray
The nights are endless, a covering black leading to day
Where the devil tap dances and waits outside my door
When I scream in defeat and can't take anymore
A furious pain travels up my chest
And I hear a voice say, "but you're not like the rest"
The load I was given is heavy as hell
It seems like voodoo or a witch's spell
On the edge and ready to quit
Right on time my angels step in
The family and friends that know my pain
And never judge, turn their heads or walk away
You're nothing short of my saving grace
When I couldn't save myself and your love stayed
I spent some time with both God and the devil
Sometimes I listen, sometimes a rebel
But what's been proven and what I see
I am loved tremendously
There is a battle between God and the devil
Where your soul and mind are up on a pedestal
And each will auction up a price
Life will take you for a ride
Be patient, take it all in stride
God always wins the war with your family and friends by your side

Angel

With wingspan outstretched enough to cover the earth
Angels are high above us just like the birds
And sometimes they are even right here amongst us
Like that stranger that helped you and offered you a hug
Or that coworker who saw you feeling blue and bought you lunch
In the Bible and Quran, angels are everywhere high and low
When you encounter one you always know
It is said we all have a guardian angel, one who is meant to guide us
Like Jibreel speaking to the prophets and the message they provide us
Or Israfeel blowing the horn on judgement day
An angel is never far away
If you close your eyes and dream
Have faith so strong, trust in God and believe
You will know it's true and you will see
Angels are earthbound and here just for you and me

Printed in the United States
By Bookmasters